# A Mosaic of Poetry and Art

*Evelyn Chubb*

## Evelyn Chubb

INFINITY
PUBLISHING

Copyright © 2010 by Evelyn Chubb

ISBN 0-7414-6090-4

Printed in the United States of America

Published  June 2010

INFINITY PUBLISHING
1094 New DeHaven Street, Suite 100
West Conshohocken, PA 19428-2713
Toll-free (877) BUY BOOK
Local Phone (610) 941-9999
Fax (610) 941-9959
Info@buybooksontheweb.com
www.buybooksontheweb.com

*With love to Suzie Christie,*
*my only child*

Sincere thanks to Suzie's husband, David Christie, who took the photographs of the paintings; and Beth Mansbridge, professional copyeditor, for the setup and editing of my book.

# Contents

### *Artwork by Evelyn Chubb*

*Pen-and-Ink Drawings, Pastels, Oils,
and Watercolor Paintings*

*Spring Aroma*

*Thoughts and Drawings*

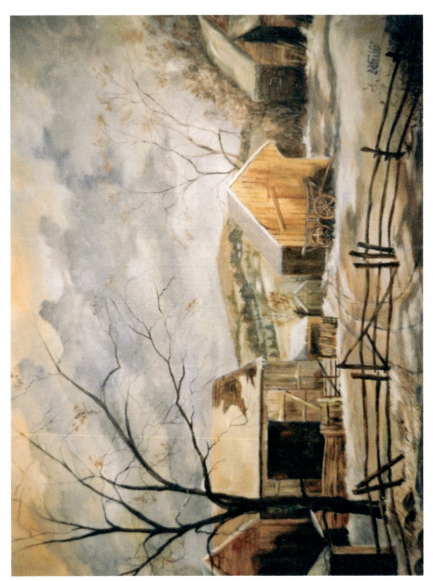

*Christie's Barn*

*Thoughts and Drawings*

# A Reflection: Sitting, Rocking, and Musing

Life seems to move on, even in retirement, at such a swift and frenetic pace. Despite having lupus and a myriad of lesser ills, I consider my lifestyle active, and find great contentment when lulled in body and spirit by the salubrious motion of a rocking chair. Rocking chairs have always held a significant place in my life, and I have been fascinated with them ever since a severely handicapped and impoverished aunt somehow managed to buy me a lovely little mahogany one for my fourth birthday. Seventy-six years later, I can still squeeze into it. I inherited two more treasured ones when my mother died, and purchased one outdoor variety for enjoying nature's delights. Currently, my two great-grandchildren rush to that little rocker in the living room and seem to enjoy it greatly.

Soothed in body and spirit by the rocking motion, I find that the somnolent "squeak, squeak" of the chair not only relaxes me, but triggers my memory in a most delightful way, allowing me to recall treasured recollections of bygone days and events.

Many years ago, just about every family in my neighborhood had rocking chairs in their front porch and entertainment on hot summer nights, and we spent time sitting, rocking, and musing. It enabled families to connect and interact so pleasantly.

Rocking is an excellent way to improve one's circulation. The "to and fro" exercise is a palliative for rheumatic pain. Perhaps you recall President Kennedy following his doctor's advice and constantly using a rocking chair for prolonged reading. Dr. Janet Travel's advice to President Kennedy had an impact on rheumatic people around the world. Changing positions relaxes one's muscles and helps in other ways. A fan from Massachusetts started an international Rocking Chair Club. One is never too old or too young to enjoy "Sitting, Rocking, and Musing."

*Thoughts and Drawings*

*A Season's Mix*

*Thoughts and Drawings*

# A Visit to the Sanctuary

I walked down the long red carpet
And slid into the second pew,
The church seemed so cool and quiet
As I bowed a prayer to YOU.

Somehow YOU seemed so different there,
I can't explain just why—
With no one else but YOU and me,
We talked, I prayed, and sighed.

I said, "When I worship on Sundays,
I look about to see
Who is in the front and back?
How pretty their hats might be."

"Next time you attend MY service,
Don't gaze and whisper, be still,
Pick up the Bible and think on it,
Then pray and surrender your will."

And then YOU spoke those lovely words
That I have heard before,
"I do not change, wherever I be,
But Christian, LOVE ME MORE."

*Thoughts and Drawings*

*Afternoon in the Woods*

*Thoughts and Drawings*

# A Woods of Our Own

Our decade's treasure trove increased,
So we could buy some land,
Oh, let it have a tree or two,
To grace the house we'd planned.

A lengthy search produced a grove,
Of tall cathedral towers,
More trees and thickets everywhere,
Could these stately woods be ours?

There were tulip poplars, mighty oaks,
And dogwood in profusion,
Enrobed in green-tipped, shadowed lace,
They welcomed our intrusion.

The ebb and flow of curving limbs,
Wove their wooden, tendriled sprays,
Through arches lattice-like in space,
In a cool and silent maze.

When trails touched our cherished hearth,
Root strength in marked degree,
Came from the tranquil toughness,
We found growing in our family tree.

*Thoughts and Drawings*

*Harmony in Black & White*

*Thoughts and Drawings*

# A Raccoon's Tale

When Daniel Boone met me,
He wasn't very fair;
He flipped his axe across my back,
And whacked off my black-ringed tail.

Then his "coonskin" cap was mighty praised,
And added to his fame,
While this raccoon sadly wonders why,
Greed is man's basic aim.

*Thoughts and Drawings*

*Oley Valley Charm*

*Thoughts and Drawings*

# Acre of Perfection

There's an acre of perfection,
Tucked deep beyond our view,
Where blends her lofty riches,
As the Master guides her through;

How like a gifted artist,
With palette close at hand,
He strokes in mighty wonder,
The beauties of this land;

I found my chosen acre,
One balmy, summer day,
My traveled trail seemed distant,
For I had lost my way.

There below me stood a cottage,
Enchanting as could be,
A thatched, straw roof to top its wall,
High, tiny panes to see.

How peaceful it lay waiting,

Like a mystic, fairy den,

Pink hollyhocks climbed here and there,

Bright bluebells clung to them;


A willow wept its ageless charm,

Into a winding stream,

I crossed its rustic, crooked bridge,

To find life's welcome dream.


What magic roamed within this fold?

Erasing the years of woe,

Now here at last about my feet,

A nurtured peace could grow.

*Thoughts and Drawings*

*Thoughts and Drawings*

# Alive Again

So suddenly you entered my life,
Like a rare, shiny comet,
When grief lay gnawing my spirit,
Your presence ignited me
And I felt Alive Again!
Now, no matter what happens next,
I'll never hear your voice without
Responding to its warm, rich timbre.
I'll always feel the magic
When your hand touches mine.
How good it is to feel ALIVE AGAIN!
All shades of your being seem
Intertwined with mine.
Echoing the palette of my life
With the tapestry of yours,
You're part of me FOREVER!

*Thoughts and Drawings*

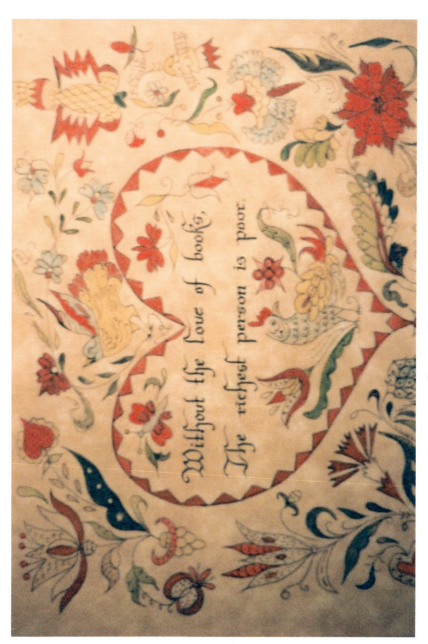

Without the love of books,
The richest person is poor.

*Lasting Bequests*

*Thoughts and Drawings*

# Crossroads of Faith

A youth stepped out in the morning of life,
So eager to conquer his way,
Knowing somewhere on a road far ahead
Lay the purpose to God's earthly day.

His struggle down life brought danger and strife,
Still the youth journeyed hopefully on,
Which guidepost would point to the
    CROSSROADS OF FAITH?
For now weary, his bright hope had gone.

One day, in despair, he prayed for God's help,
Then offered to Him his whole heart,
Only this led straight to the
    CROSSROADS OF FAITH,
Where the seed of life's service must start.

*Thoughts and Drawings*

*The Holy Truth*

*Thoughts and Drawings*

# Every Man's Jury

Every man's mind is a jury,
That stands on trial with his life,
The Scale of Justice is balanced within,
By the weight of his struggles and strife;
Not all would condemn a lawless deed—
Or a heart that proved proud and unkind,
Each may defend his pureness of thought,
Still the verdict is ruled by the mind.
Perhaps it's best that man stands accused,
Apart from the judgment of men,
There meets his counsel, the inner self,
To plead for his freedom again;
The tread of conscience is weak or strong,
Tied many ways by the past,
So it seems every man must forgive and forget—
Or his mold to Insanity is cast.

*Thoughts and Drawings*

*Best of Friends*

*Thoughts and Drawings*

# Gift of a Day

There seems the greatest treasure,
In the gift of each new day,
With chance to cancel old mistakes,
And time to chart new ways.

If only for an hour,
Some truth grows still more clear,
Then we should be so hopeful,
For there's greater wisdom near.

I know no finer reason,
To wake to morning light,
Than just the bright, rich promise,
God guides us on till night.

He lifts our eyes to beauty,
So we might see, like He,
And fills our cup with courage,
For whatever toil might be.

We cannot be discouraged,
Though troubles mount on high,
For God grants His Kingdom freely,
To the likes of you and I.

*Thoughts and Drawings*

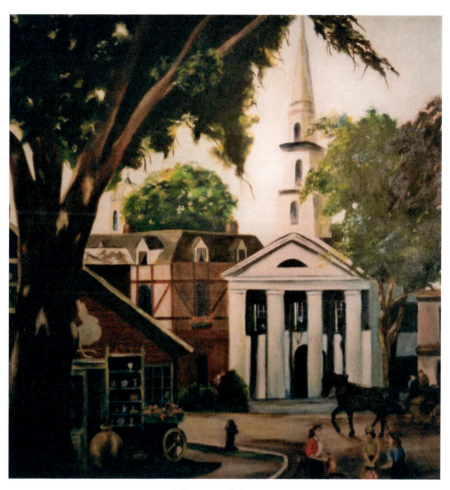

*A Spiritual Retreat*

*Thoughts and Drawings*

# Just a Thank You

God guided my path to your little church

And assured me that very first day,

That here all his people were friendly and warm

When a stranger passed by their way.


But never a stranger was I made to feel,

So wide was your welcoming heart,

You richened my faith and strengthened my hope,

Till it saddens me now to part.


I leave with a prayer of humble thanks

For the kind fellowship you have shown,

Here I have known a oneness with Christ

And a new inner peace all my own.

*Thoughts and Drawings*

*Teenage Sparkle*

*Thoughts and Drawings*

# The Golden Road

Across the continent of FEAR,
Springs forth the country, DOUBT,
There, nestled in the storm-tossed hills,
All troubles loom about;

So tarry not with FEAR and DOUBT,
When you travel the lifetime way,
But search instead for the Golden Road,
And you'll find the brighter day.

It separates the mountain of FAITH,
From the beautiful garden of LOVE,
There nestled lies a fountain of HOPE,
With a flow of PEACE from above.

Do not despair when your feet seem lost,
And your eyes can't find their way,
For always, night seems so very dark,
Before the first break of day;

The quest for a treasure is always long,
And exacts its measured price,
But for those with a farseeing heart and eye,
Just a glimpse of gold will suffice.

Now choose dear God as your steadfast guide,
Pack FAITH and HOPE for supply,
Let LOVE go ahead and light the path,
And set your goals to the sky.

It won't be long till a day will dawn,
When the Golden Road looks clear,
Beyond you've found the beautiful way,
Then the highest in life lies near.

*A Wintry Mix*

*Thoughts and Drawings*

## The Little Brown Rocker

The little brown rocker lived all alone,

In a corner of the attic stair,

And try as she might to be happy and bright,

Her "Evelyn" forgot she was there;

Each morning, the little brown rocker wished hard,

That "Evelyn" would come for her soon,

To take her out to the sunny white porch,

And rock and rock her till noon;

One day the scream of her voice

Echoed high to her attic dome,

And the lashing brakes of a passing car—

Left the little brown rocker alone;

Long days and weeks, then years passed by,

The little brown rocker grew old,

Her shiny brown varnish now peeled and dull,

Had left her tired and cold;

But saddest of all was her aching heart,

So longing for help from above,

Each night, she rocked a prayer to God,

"Please send me some love."

One morning, she heard the sound of steps,

Hobbling their way to the stair,

Then looked in sad eyes of a little brown face,

At her poor, crippled legs, with care;

They both were brown and both were sad,

And both in need of a friend,

So together they rocked and together they laughed,

And lived there happy to the end.

*Array of Forsythia*

*Thoughts and Drawings*

# The Sunlit Way

How gay the bright, rich sunlight
Dances on its merry way,
Then skips to scale the treetops
To plan a busy day.

It spins a path of magic,
The like of golden thread,
And shimmers warmest greetings
To hurry out of bed.

Each lovely flower beckons
A welcome to their friend,
The sun, in happy answer,
Lights down its warmth to blend.

So joyful in their kinship,
They spread their glory round,
The birds and bees soon gather
In chorus of gleeful sound.

All natures then responding,

The call of the glowing sun,

Seeing between the sunbeams,

The smile of the HOLY ONE.


I, too, thrive in this wonder

That marks the glorious day.

Throw open my heart in thanksgiving,

To absorb "The Sunlit Way."

*Lasting Beauty*

*Thoughts and Drawings*

# The Tender Touch

Oh! The source of a woman's delight,

Bargain sale in the paper last night:

The flash of excitement bursts into mind,

At the thought of treasures, with luck, I'll find.

My greatest obstacle now lies in view,

How to procure the money I'm due.

I see my kind husband in his favorite chair,

Oh! He looks so harmless relaxing there.

Gathering all feminine wiles in hand,

I lovingly, sweetly, make my demand,

Oh! For a camera to record his surprise,

And register the dollar mark signs in his eyes.

With typical masculine logic he speaks,

"You've overspent your allowance for weeks."

Now banding together my courage to say,

"But look at the money I've saved you this way."

Oh why! Oh why! Can't men ever see

How wise and thrifty we women can be?

He cynically shakes his tired old head,

Hands me his wallet and crawls off to bed.

I think to myself—how lucky is he,

To have a wife manage money like me.

*Thoughts and Drawings*

*North to Alaska*

*Thoughts and Drawings*

*Thoughts and Drawings*

*Langhorne Neighbors*

*Thoughts and Drawings*

*Favorite Blue Onion Dishes*

*Thoughts and Drawings*

# The Wise Surveyor

WISE SURVEYOR of all my life,
What have Thou seen in me?
For while my lips vow steadfast faith,
A glimpse within shows me to Thee:

I need not tell of lofty goals;
The hours wasted in prideful gain,
While I reveled my selfish joys,
Thou waiting in pitying pain;

Dear WISE SURVEYOR, believe in me,
When You search throughout my heart,
Please see a soul that longs to serve,
Where no burden would tear us apart;

In reverent steps, Thou planted my life,
With a goal of splendor in mind,
Transform this self to Thy gloried will,
Then mold me blessedly Thine.

*Thoughts and Drawings*

*Evelyn's Treasured Gift*

69

*Thoughts and Drawings*

# You Know Who He Is

He walks among us with a prayer,
This great and humble man,
Witnessing CHRIST in spoken word,
With a doctrine of love in his hand.

Boldly and firmly, yet so gently too,
He shares all the roots of our strife,
Ever pleading for full commitments,
Teaching, "CHRIST is the armor of life."

Yet do we thank him nearly enough,
For the faith he lives to the letter?
And because he came to serve our church,
We now know our Savior better.

Composed in tribute to our beloved minister,
Rev. Carl Hammerly

*Thoughts and Drawings*

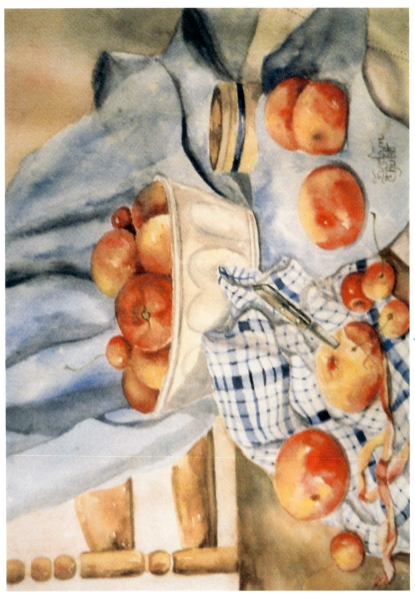

*A Composite in Blue*

*Thoughts and Drawings*

# Seeking the Afterglow

I wonder …?

Are all my halcyon days forever past?

As crumbling bones and infections sting,

Cold metal cage and cane direct my steps.

A maelstrom swarms around me!

Is sickness now entrenched within?

Surely some potent interloper has usurped my very spirit.

What has happened to the joyous person I once knew?

Harking back to my salad days,

Fervently wanting to exceed my limits,

Now I no longer fit into this world of speed!

Nothing is going to vanquish me!

I am a Child of the King, and with God's help,

I can still do wondrous things.

Maybe not walk well, but I am seeking still—

And I will find the "Afterglow."

*Thoughts and Drawings*

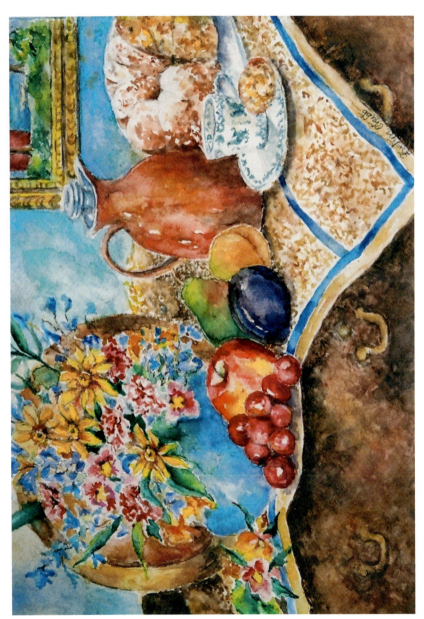

*Tea Time*

*Thoughts and Drawings*

# The Flu

You gifted me with fever's flush,
And gurgling fluid in the chest.
Then listened while my racking cough,
Sent dissonant cadence to the test.
In rueful taunts of evil glee,
You fiendishly jeered, "Now suffer, you SHE."
From the chills and sneezing weakness,
Coughed my anguished, pitiful plea,
"Let loose this grip of torture,
I must be well and free."
My week is stamped with glowing affairs,
In numbers, a dizzying array,
A party, a lecture, a birthday, all three,
Two bridge games, an art class, a luncheon, you see.
My pleadings ignored, with malevolent cool,
"YOU" marked CANCELLED across my calendar's rule.
So here I toss, watery red of eye,
Profusion of tissues collecting, I sigh,
What can I do while lying here so supine?
Toe into my extremity, and pen a little rhyme.

*Grandma's Pantry*

*Thoughts and Drawings*

# My Home

I found a very lovely home,
Yet strange it is indeed,
For though it has no walls or room,
It fulfills my deepest need;

It knows no single limit bound,
By ceiling or by floor,
Yet rambles on for many a mile,
No queen could ask for more;

It guards me from the world outside,
Still brings the whole world in,
And imparts a special inner sight,
To love each Godly thing;

My home is restful, warm, and strong,
Gentle laughter all around,
No need for surging, troubled fears,
Within, it tempers all my cares.

My home is not an idle dream,
That never could come true,
For dearest darling of my heart,
My lovely home is YOU!

*Thoughts and Drawings*

*My Teenage Daughter*

*Thoughts and Drawings*

# My Teenage Daughter

My teenage daughter thinks I'm such fun,
That is, until some work must be done,
Then grimacing wildly, she calls me unfair,
"You give me too many burdens to bear."

How slowly the vacuum moves on its way,
In her struggle to still hear the radio play,
Above the din, she makes a mad dash,
Is there by the phone, quick as a flash.

How long she may talk, fades completely from mind,
A half-hour later she's still deeply entwined,
We finally rule her to "ten-minute" talks,
Rebelling her plight, out the back door she walks.

Returning transformed, I can tell by her smile,
That the boy down the street made her walk so worthwhile;

The greatest grievance she gives me by far,

Is the time I'm kept waiting while chauffeuring her car,

I drop her off here and pick her up there

As she blithely departs with nary a care.


Still, in counting the joys she brings me each day,

Then tells me she loves me in her sweet, special way,

I think of her faults, how meager they seem,

For in facing the facts, my daughter's a Dream.


With a glance in the mirror to survey this gray hair,

It reminds me what fun we had putting it there.

*Thoughts and Drawings*

*Thoughts and Drawings*

# Noisy Assaults

I am a friend of silence,

Trapped in the clamoring coil of life,

Yet seeking the placid quietude of painting and book,

While the shriek of jet and roar of truck

Rumble their piston and ring,

In ever nerve-racking plentitude.

Oh, for the calming quiet of noiseless hours,

To ponder the sweet build-up of untested thought.

The clash and grate of internal dissonance

Assault these noise-ravaged ears.

No air of tranquility reposes here.

THE WORLD IS OFF KEY.

We're lost in a battleground of decibels.

No escape from the blaring babble of radio and TV,

No reprieve from the tuneless canticles of mower, saw,

and cycle,

No deliverance from the drag-strip clatters of washer

and dryer,

No avoidance of hearing loss from this cacophony of noise,

Our lot is lost—all in the pursuit of progress.

PLEASE BE QUIET!

*Thoughts and Drawings*

*Celebrating Daffodils*

*Thoughts and Drawings*

# Consolation

Why worry if your mirror
Records deep lumps of fat.
It could be that old mirror
Can't see too well, at that.

*Thoughts and Drawings*

*Hands of Faith*

*Thoughts and Drawings*

# Easter Morning

When one awakes on Easter,
God's world seems somehow new,
For round about the flowers bloom
In a more radiant hue.

No day exacts more glory,
Than a lovely Easter morn,
For stirring in the heart of man,
Springs hope to be reborn.

All nature reigns in splendor,
In tribute to our King,
Who, rising from the darkest tomb,
Defeated Death's sharp sting.

Then too, on Easter morning,
My Savior walks close by,
And in the warmth of sunshine,
He smiles a joyful sigh.

His whisper breathes a promise,
"Come now and follow Me.
For in my Resurrected Life,
You share Eternity."

*Thoughts and Drawings*

*Snack Time*

*Thoughts and Drawings*

# Spiritual Millionaire

I became a millionaire today.
You say that cannot be.
But I can prove my riches,
They dwell inside of me.

Though the future looms in shadow,
My wealth could greater grow,
For a storehouse of the spirit
Will reap what I can sow.

Inside are heaped the blessings
My God has shared with me.
I pray to be most worthy
Of this richest trust for Thee.

The world is mine for keeping
From each morn till closing night,
Then I gather up my harvest
To place in tomorrow's light.

If all the seeming paupers
Would look within they'd see
Their mounting, unclaimed blessings,
Then all millionaires we'd be.

*Thoughts and Drawings*

*Thoughts and Drawings*

*"Skip" the Squirrel*

*Thoughts and Drawings*

*Thoughts and Drawings*

*Thoughts and Drawings*

*Thoughts and Drawings*

Evelyn Chubb, Author and Artist

# *About the Author-Artist*

Evelyn Chubb was born in the heart of Pennsylvania—Dutchland—in Reading. Her German mother, Beulah Berstler, and Greek father, Andrew Cassimatis, were divorced when Evelyn was a young girl. Both parents were diligent workers at the Crystal Restaurant, a landmark on Penn Street. Evelyn was often left alone while her parents struggled seven days a week to make a living. During those lonely hours she wrote poetry, painted pictures, created dresses for her paper dolls, and pretended to be a movie star.

Her sixth-grade teacher, Miss Strunk, inspired Evelyn to become a teacher. Evelyn married Dick Chubb, an excellent football player and golfer, who taught radio and television at Temple University. At the age of nineteen, Evelyn gave birth to Suzie, her only child.

After Suzie graduated from college, Evelyn pursued her dream of obtaining her master's degree in English literature, and she has 60 credits towards her doctorate. Evelyn taught English at Bensalem High School in Bucks County, Sunday school classes at Langhorne Methodist Church, and offered art classes in her home to adults and children.

Along with her poems, the pages of *A Mosaic of Poetry and Art* are illustrated with her original pen-and-ink drawings, pastels, oils, and watercolor paintings which have won many awards at local competitions in Berks Country, Pennsylvania.

She has been a docent at the Reading Museum and a member of Toastmasters. As her preferred pastimes she lists playing duplicate bridge, painting, and creative writing. Presently, Evelyn is trying to remain independent but her arthritis and lupus are making the aging process a challenge.

When Evelyn lived in North Carolina, her friend and president of the Poetry Society, Emily Councilman, told her, "Promise me you won't die before you publish your poetry." Evelyn is realizing her dream. This is Evelyn's first publication of poetry in 86 years and it is her hope that it will bring joy to all who read it.